Written by : NEIL ORRIDGE

E-mail : neilorridge13@gmail.com

First printed in 2022 by Suraj industries (India)
+91 93153 05660

Index

CRYBABY

Introduction

There are no monsters here. There's just things that became thoughts. Messiahs and miseries, now memoirs and memories. There's my words... Now yours.

There are no monsters here.
There's just us, crybabies.

I like it when an experience has stayed around long enough to create a contrasting tension between the way it appeared initially and what remains of it now. Tension between the way I once took care of it and the way it'll be cared for by someone else now.

Crybaby is just that...

A collection of experiences, thoughts, memories: treasures eccentric, small-scale, maybe a little rusty and run down... But human, nonetheless.

What do I want to say with Crybaby?

Honour the human in you. Celebrate yourself. Care brings hardship. The person you nurtured yourself into was cared for... Not by hardship... but, by you.

There are no monsters here. Just the human in me and you.

Crybaby is remnants of those human memories. Marks made by me. Somewhere, made by you too.

Memories flowing through battered old porches, still beaches, porcelain statues, quiet and cosy balconies. Words whispering remnants of me and I hope somewhere in here there's too whispers of you.

There are no monsters here...

Just us, cry babies.

Loss, Therapy... Depression...

As I was with the blade in my hand...
Scarlet sulk grieved to bathe the blade-end...
Whispers of crimson comfort with new talks...
Claret of clarity regrets staining the tablecloth...
Converse of the cover chauffeurs the table's tounge dumb...
To verse the ballad of old bruises...
Narrating new numb...
Christens this corner with cold...
Sepia toned this scenery brush-stroked with silences sullen...
Sudden this stifle brings shivers talkative...
But oh do I bring the burn...
Forsake fuels the creed keeping this candle kindled...
Where the kiss of its wick hot-lipped burns the air out of my lungs...
Wrung wrinkled off the tar of memories tormenting...
Till short breaths wheeze mentions of dead friends...
Breathing murmurs of a sweet child losing life against sick snake like...
I wonder if this is the tranquil of therapy they so religiously suggest..?
I wonder if this is... Help...
Creaking seats empty try and tell me to fill in the gaps...
Acquiescent, this touch of anxiety gives company...
But, sloughs off my skin with each caress...
Body becomes a cell prisonless...
Barred with peace prisoning that my blade won't cut through...
Cold sweat combines with shortened breaths...
Perturbed, my pulse increases pace...
To escape gazes petrifying of the ghosts of lost kin... And so their embrace...
Forces faith in the fabled flesh untainted...
To face the abyss flushed skin...
With a single candle flame in hand to make this eternal path pitch dark...
Somehow, candlelit...
Surfaces sick under eyelids...
Fingers twitch losing touch with life...
Blood leaves body when tears of red run down wrists slit...
And where sick breaks skin, grow newer daffodils of confess...
And then...

Even the candle-light critiques my silhouette...
It's depression... Darling...
Depression...
So biting my nape with pity won't help bleed the sick out of my sinew...
It'll just mark me velvet with another lyric of self-loathing... Wound me with its peck...
As flesh invites teeth deeper inside...
Just to feel something...
And oh do I hate that feeling...
For, I fear what I feel will force the part of "other" to be known...
So, I gut myself a new lover in reminisce when reason leaves me home...
Remembrance allows refuge in mind...
Then remind, burial grounds muted...
That I'm alone...
And laden me with their dull hush eternal to listen to... Coupled with my own whine incandescent...
First, this sombre deafens...
Then buries the sting with lack of sleep...
Till thoughts intrusive further worsen...
And concrete completely coffins body...
And introspection envelopes person...
Health worsens and riches rust...
And where remains dust instead of kingdom... I sit to navel-gaze...
But, wherein I ruminate muses newer evils within my womb...
So, I rip this rhythm...
And eat out its cunt...
I hate the way it hums... This window...
Carolling the cold wind's prose...
Blowing it's bustle behind the blinds...
Whilst calloused this sill, sits still...
Taunting the traffic's biting brisk with silence so solemn...

Keep on keeping on!

Suggesting...
I'm better off an orphan...
So I severe my bonds...
Coercing the curtains to close...
Making newer friends with the cobwebs of conflict sprawling underneath this table too loudly...
Infested with conversations well versed with oneself... left unheard by the others...
The symphony of scorn they sing does my ears no favours...
Each chord discoursing my depression chronic...
Like feather stems forced through my temples...
Tied tight to my throat, this contempt...
Marionettes me with tenacity...
But, I swear this isn't a talent...
Just discontent of iring intensity...
And the form rustling behind the blinds...
Is of those that now aren't next to me...
So, compensating...
There I was... With the blade in my hand...
And the tears on my sleeve still feared tugs of repent...
And underneath kissed wrist scars of attempts....
Cuts replaced lullabies of care hummed by kin...
Calm composed itself still...
And even stiller, this chill killed tender from touch...
Till bonds bruised skin...
But, don't worry darling...
There's always a farce to foreclose old thoughts... And so forgo old sins...
And since, I've played the victim for long...
I'll now be playing... unhinged...
Don't worry darling...
I'll be seeing the end of this...
Even if I don't win...

An Apostle's Date ...

I wonder what remains of me..?

Perhaps, a postulate picketing his presaged purgatory...

For, picking me this evening is another promised periphery...

You see, I've a date pre-established... Just never agreed...

So please, for me...

Pray, prophecy's a better usher... Atleast, for this eve...

So now, being chauffeured around in what roughly resembles Providence...

I'd say its comfortable this crusade...

Though on top of the tired tires of penitence fringing the rusty run down rims of a role predetermined...

This wheel of life struggles to spin...

But at least... keeps moving...

Once shimmering, this role traded its silver for riddles of rust, riddling slivers of hope...

First, struggling up the steep road they reckon destiny.... then against it's even steeper downslope...

The rust it now gropes is of its own failed acceptance as a niche...

But to digress...

Isn't it cosy, this backseat..?

And from here, the one chauffeuring me seems to be... Fortuity..?

Fortune's most favoured child...

A fluke famed infamous...

Whilst, unnamed this rear view mirror reckons, the least favoured child is me...

Blurry, this windshield keeps ballading the evenfall's venue in visions...

Though, I'd rather trust the tire in my eyes...

And their retinas reflecting the burnt in image of a destination predestined...

Keep on keeping on!

I wonder what remains of me..?
Perhaps, a postulate picketing his presaged purgatory...
For, picking me this evening is another promised periphery...
You see, I've a date pre-established... Just never agreed...
So please, for me...
Pray, prophecy's a better usher... Atleast, for this eve...
So now, being chauffeured around in what roughly resembles Providence...
I'd say its comfortable this crusade...
Though on top of the tired tires of penitence fringing the rusty run down rims of a role predetermined...
This wheel of life struggles to spin...
But at least... keeps moving...
Once shimmering, this role traded its silver for riddles of rust, riddling slivers of hope...
First, struggling up the steep road they reckon destiny.... then against it's even steeper downslope...
The rust it now gropes is of its own failed acceptance as a niche...
But to digress...
Isn't it cosy, this backseat..?
And from here, the one chauffeuring me seems to be... Fortuity..?
Fortune's most favoured child...
A fluke famed infamous...
Whilst, unnamed this rear view mirror reckons, the least favoured child is me...
Blurry, this windshield keeps ballading the evenfall's venue in visions...
Though, I'd rather trust the tire in my eyes...

And their retinas reflecting the burnt in image of a destination predestined...

For, at least they see what's real...

And not what they're told to perceive being reality...

And seeing how forethought never allowed me any room for heresy... Or for that matter freethinking...

I'd like to think there's more to my gaze's reneging than "mere" peeks allowing leers at glories trifling cuddling clichés of recreance's pillaging...

And that, piercing the haze blinked into existence by the eyelashes aloft the leers, beyond appears, future foresight foretelling messiahs... From miseries...

Well, being as heathens have no messiahs to believe in...

I suppose I'll make my religion my own recusant creativity...

So I'm free to wonder what table awaits me...

Reckon, a space sparkling pristine...

Cluttered with the cutlery of fables unused...

Perhaps too...

Covered by a tablecloth cautiously stained in luxury... Much less embroidered with devout...

Though, I suppose now...

Already sat atop my seat, this chill, spilling sharp from this cranny crisp...

Isn't exactly the eminence exemplary I'd expected...

Nor the experience for me this evening had scripted...

Or so it seems... Evidently...

Atleast, the food looks fancy... Right..?

But curated exquisite this cuisine, doesn't just taste bland... But also bleak...

I guess, it's true after all...

Clockwork...

Won't you slow down...
Sit still for a while...
I know you can't ever wait around...
Nor can you ever smile...
The monotony you tick-tock...
Titillates time... Just enough to induce a sigh...
This eternal efficiency you sound...
For a wordless clock...
Sounds infinitely vile...
I think, you're much too loud...
For a timepiece twinkling with only a closure serene to perpetually offer...
Your talks are too continual for my taste...
But, atleast keeping me manicured there's always the unsettling edge they author...
Snipped stubby till I bite skin...
Comically, it's such shabby clockwork that's eternal...
Whilst eternity for me, twins the trancience ticking from this mechanism manic...
And residing therein, this temporality...
Only ever has my youth timelessly painted... curling off...
And narrating stories irrelevant...
Graffitied, my resolve... Hides in each slough forlorn...
For long...
Had i walked this colourful path, you'd so ambitiously spawned...
But now, taunting me to tilt my head a little, this corner constantly echoing your far cry...
Forces me to see this path so brittle, crippled, under it's true shade...
As a religious stain tailing conclusions forgone...
And not the canvas painted with finesse I'd taken it for...

CRYBABY

So, obviously now...
Animating this cranny whilst hanging lifeless...
The eternity you hum...
To me, no longer sounds like a hymn immortal... Just immutable...
But, I digress...
For, you never left me with enough time to allow myself reflection... Or for that matter rest...
You see...
The moments you offer saunter too subtly...
For you to call this play, a crusade...
And this chant you charade, although ceaseless itself...
Now blockades too persistently my parade...
So, I'll just force upon you a corner...
Entrap you, using the exact crippled chronology you utter as bait...
So, when I stumble round the clock, fumbling through fate...
You have a moment of stillness...
So quiet and cosy...
In this newfound place...
With even newer silence... To overstay...

Talk of the Town ...

Don't worry wanderer...
Lift up your eyes from the ground...
Your stare now feels tired...
Weightless in its touch acquiescent...
Yet, this caress with reminisce feels much too weighed down...
There's safety in fear...
When it's the stone not the grave you're looking upon...
There's significance in the names...
Not the expired egos or the plenty dirt dug around...
It's heaven they offer...
And not the puddles of grave plots...
Reflecting your presence muzzled...
Muddled in mire, singing your muffled renown...
Perhaps, when you'll be leaving tomorrow...
You'll come to appreciate the beauty in this sound...
Maybe tomorrow...
You'll be the talk of the town...
A puzzle piece in disconnect does the grander picture no favours...
Suppose, what creates the distance is this discontent..?
Reckon, nearing death we'd finally be able to lose all its fear...
Only to instead start fearing insignificance...
Twining your head around this question in twain...
You question why condemns you this contempt perpetual...
Don't worry wanderer...
Maybe tomorrow...
Life will seem more like a journey...
And less like a ritual...
A ritual, where we peruse distinction...
Till the day we're either subtly sedimented...
Or in a pyre, as mere ashen residual...
Whines your ego for noteworthiness...
Till the ire, it leeches off your sinew it's substance...
Plucked your lust for life from within you...

Keep on keeping on!

This fire for living... So fervent...
You see...
Suggests this fire, set ablaze, redundant, your aim can only ever ask for the same old chase...
One that's after the same old burn...
Burning the same old bright...
Just each time, coloured a little different...
And so, suggesting the same...
There's too, the rest aflame...
Indifferent, if not a little cosied by this chaos...
You assert what they admire isn't eternity...
But, fame endless...
Though, assertions as such shan't ever be made by liers with conscience...
For, you see, an assertion of the sort won't really be a lie...
Especially, if it's just the truth... contorted...
And oh well, there's always this reason governing, why remains unassertive, the faceless friend you seek amidst the townsmen...
Contortive...
The dear liers are cunning, cursing out contemplation in cursive...
Putting pretty bows atop heads mangled...
So you can see the woes wording your scorn...
As poetry petite, worth it...
Don't worry wanderer...
Past the malice in the lies you'll find greed...
But, surely somewhere even past that...
There's comfort... Coloured the right coercive...
The artifact named anxiety...
Makes for the altar baptizing you nameless...
The town's reject...
Filling grounds forsaken and emptiness idle, abandoned there lies the altar of your home...
And to rely upon there's always its neighbour... Neglect...

Keep on keeping on!

Chastity hides in its shadow...
And so hides the desertion chastising it...
The living space inside stifles your breath...
Perhaps, this feeling of frivolity wouldn't have been a concept so foreign...
If you weren't breathing under the roof of a forgotten wilt...
Hushes this environment, the raining droplets of quiet...
And it's almost serene, this stillness...
Until comes crashing down the rain, breaking the cracked glass panels of tranquil...
And so, breaking the silence...
Cosies it, its own colourlessness...
Almost lucent, especially when paired against the familiar backdrop of blackness condensed...
Ironic, how a speck so colourless for long had carried the scenery's prominence...
That was, until your passion painted it lurid...
Completes the scenery, the frontier complimented alongside it...
Separating the talkative town from the peaceful putrid...
The river Styx, with all its candescence latex...
And there lies you...
Pedaling against it...
Though, I suppose, when it all comes around being acknowledged as trivial would still have been an acknowledgement...
Don't worry wanderer...
Cries the town for you after all...
Hush them, waving goodbyes in silence, ever so sound...
A lullaby for sirens...
So, when you'll be leaving tomorrow...
They'll blow kisses to you till the sun's going down...
So, leaving tomorrow...
You'll be the talk of the town...
It's almost tomorrow...

The serpent named... Cancer

Fear...
It's the apple nourishing the cancer...
Embalming it's decay inciting memory...
As it dances with its devilish grin amongst the sloughed frills of life...
Of a child... Barely four...
The offence of fear...
And you... Oh accuser...
Cancer...
You're a molting snake...
Feeding off the child's skin...
Whilst you try escaping your own...
I abhor you...
Akin to the abhorrent succubus...
Your sin was being a life stealing whore...
Your sin was stealing... Her...
Selua...
I adore you... Selua...
For being a symbol of life...
Bannering hope against the rioting winds of
despair...
And oh did the winds riot...
In the temple of man that was the hospital room...
When the capricious climate calloused...
As the priest donning the doctor's robe...
Chanted at us...
The uninvited answer...
That your sanctuary could no longer withstand the slander...
The slander accused by the accuser... Cancer...
His words eddied around my stormy seas...
Where the oar of hope I once held onto tight...
Subsided into the pearled droplets of tears...

The serpent named... Cancer

The tears of despair... Of fright...
Seeping from my hands into the sea...
Repleting the unrelenting waves... of repent...
At least I still had a boat...
Though brimful of holes and lacking an oar...
At Least I still had a boat... In you laughter...
Your laughter kept us afloat...
Conquering the sea, it rode...
Giggling life into the cacophony...
Lullabied by the storm's lifeless prose...
It kept me from drowning...
Or struggling on the sea's surface...
Be it false hope... It apprised me of a distant shore's grace...
It was better than drowning...
Atleast, I could sleep...
To your laughter...
Atleast, I knew...
The shore existed...
Or so I had hoped...
Maybe it was about time god showed up...
To edify this wavering day...
But, he didn't...
I suppose, it was because we both were starved for the unknown...
Maybe we never knew him enough for him to immure our plight...
To immure your Cancer...
But... We never needed him...
Even though the doctor wearing the reaper's robe... Knocked vehemently outside our hospital room's door...
If I just held you tight enough...

The serpent named... Cancer

If I just held you close...
Nothing could steal you from me... Right..?
So there we were...
And the discord we found in the misty song of the sea had finally faded into silence...
And so did you...
And the air felt emptier without your laugh...
Yet my heart was still full...
But, with a different drink...
I now sit here alone... In this new silence...
Waiting, for the song to start again...
For at least I'd be saved from the sea's rasping by the refuge in your laughter...
At least you'd still be laughing here on earth... And not just in heaven...
Though, I sense your silence here is only because you're drawing a breath peaceful...
On the shore...
And that in your next breath...
You will whisper your radiance through your laughter into the world...
Into my world...
I now grieve in silence... But, not without your presence...
Find your home on the shore, sweet child...
You are free...

Just enough...

I wonder how we came about...
Perhaps, prophecy beheld us meant to be..?
When the universe uttered life into the vacuum of it's navel...
In an outburst that stuttered time...
In the crux of its nucleus...
The mighty flux, that birthed us...
Where we found refuge in the grey of a floating rock...
The same rock, later painted blue...
The same rock we gave colour...
I find myself in dissent from this idea...
I don't believe in our decent from the heavens...
Into the omphalos of this cosmos...
I don't believe we move all of creation...
With the life in our shadows...
Silhouetted against the stars...
Dancing in the light...
Sprinkled across the macrocosm...
I don't believe we're that special...
I believe...
We're just enough...
What's momentous to me...
Is just another moment to the other...
We can't find uniqueness in the outstanding...
When even the outstanding is painted the same colour...
We're all great at being ordinary...
But, we're exceptional at being singular...
I'm not distinctive in the crowds of many...
Yet, I'm distinct at being an individual...
And that's...
Just enough...
I'm just as afraid of being a frivolous dink in the grand scheme of things...
As the many, casted upon the same shade as me...

Keep on keeping on!

CRYBABY

But, I'm happy...
I'm happy as nothing's expected of me...
I'm happy just being...
The universe's...
Another consequential kink...
I'm happy being me...
And that's just enough...
I'm not the protagonist of my own universe...
But, I'm happy just having been a peasant pawned to it...
I can choose to pawn for a king...
But even the king serves as a mere conduit...
To the ebb and flow flushed across the firmament...
The firmament that sees the king's crown as a fool's cap...
As his royal mantle makes him appear a curtain constrained clown to it...
I'm not just happy...
I'm drawn to it...
I'm happy having been drawn in it's image...
I'm happy greeting the day that never wishes back...
Under the warmth of a sun that doesn't radiate for me...
I'm happy leaving my footprints on the ground...
That never once felt... the weight of me...
I'm happy just being a corpse in the making...
A corpse that at least gets to recite his glee...
I'm happy... Being me...
And that's... Just enough...
I'm not special...
I'm just another nomad...
I'm not special...
Because everybody's just that...
I'm not special...
Because everybody is...
And that's...
Just enough...

Keep on keeping on!

The Clementine Shore...

I'm standing on the shore...
As I watch the sun burrow down...
Following the horizon's now...
A sky of gore...
The waves, they clash against the clouds...
The heavens wear this battlefield's shroud...
In dissonance to the peace whispered a little before...
The peace enchanted by the clementine shore...
I feel resonance with the sun...
Losing it's battle against the world's attrition...
For, I too am now a king without his clementine throne...
Is this my one true home..?
A warfare inside of my head...
fared off against the steps...
Tread upon the unfairness, to myself I've shown...
How did I end up all alone..?
The clementine peace is now all gone...
I'm stranded, with my hollow bones...
Planted, deep inside the only land I've ever known...
The land of my thoughts...
The land entranced plenty with vain holes...
Empty, with only the cacophonous mist that controls...
Everything stood for by my soul...
The mist... I've made a sovereign...
To this land of my woes...
This shore...
It's filled by my doubt's fountain...
The one I'd roundabout, turning moe hills into mountains...
The one, I drowned my youth inside to rebound and...
Never once I realised...

CRYBABY

My sound beliefs were the ones shouting the loudest...
Did I allow this..?
Was I the one to turn this beautiful and divine clementine shore...
Into this spineless battlefield's valentine...
Into the spineless battlefield's whore?!
Declining it's shine, blind eyed...
The shine, these eyes of mine once adored..?
It's become eminent...
I've made fear so prevalent...
The fear's numbed my beliefs...
And now my faith has become irrelevant...
My sentiments...
They're desolate even in decadence...
Of fear veiled mountains...
My soul reckons its only residence...
The leavened lesson is...
It's evident...
With eminence we command the biggest war we ever waged...
The war waged upon our own brains...
Where we build our very own effigies...
Representing the pain unseen...
Residing in the duality...
Of the thoughts we believe bleed glory into the vain...
The thoughts we bleed into the drain...
Praying to the gods with both of our hands nailed...
Nailed to this ground of self disdain...
This ground, it holds the crucifix of my effigy...
Burning, in the flames of my thoughts...
Dangling, off the noose with no support...
As the noose is made into a rosary...
Worn around the neck of this...
Clementine shore...

Maybe another life...

Remind me...
I'm scared of life...
Remind me of my fears...
The deeper I plunge...
Descending into this sludge...
Of the swamps of my failures...
Where... the thicker the muck...
The more congealed my trust...
Trust... In panic...
Trust... in the fabled rose...
Adding colour to my muddy episodes...
Manic...
It's fables birthed from the prose...
The same prose that birthed me nameless...
Where, the touch of its thorns...
Caresses my woes...
As I bleed on the gunk...
And the sedimented ground, it names me...
Heinous...
It was a deal, really...
Where the dirty sludge of this swamp...
Becomes dirtier, mixing with the curse in my blood...
Where I sell my prisoned freedom...
For a name spelt out by the mud...
Where I peruse the calm in the midst of chaos...
In my loss that occurs...
When my yin-yang muse into unison...
When I lose the duality...
In the bipolar poles of my world of fiction...
Remind me...

CRYBABY

Maybe another li

In another life...
How I cloaked my being in those fables...
Hiding from a reality pricier than the fare of fiction...
How I starved myself of belief...
When I became a glutton for punishment...
How my conviction became my plea...
How my plea became a commitment...
A plea for my release...
Seeking freedom from this malediction...
Remind me...
In another life...
I'm cursed...
Cursed by my mortality...
Imbursed by my needless contrition...
How I'm deprived of clarity...
Surprised by my own attrition...
How the impairment's become the fee...
For my journey towards fulfillment...
Remind me...
In another life...
True fulfilment doesn't exist...
The fabled rose doesn't exist...
And...
Maybe, another life doesn't... Either...
Remind me...
I'm scared of life...
Remind me...
I've strength to find...
In the fables of the fabled rose...
That maybe... another life...
Remind me...
To close my eyes...

Meridian ...

You deserve to be loved...
You can't hate yourself happy...
You can't shame yourself worthy...
You chant blame of which you're unworthy...
Glistening, with the tears that you impearled...
Can you see the meridian... you cursed..?
The meridian's now immersed...
Seeping deep into your world...
Becoming a noose that consumes...
Tied up high, it's the only thing beaming...
In your inky sky's ceiling...
The only ceiling, your epiphanies seemingly ever sung...
You can't find healing...
If you can't find meaning...
But, even blind-eyed you can spy...
Your meridian, stealing...
The life off of your lungs...
You're not cursed...
You're just depleted, you're wrung.....
There'd again be life in your breathing...
If only you'd realise...
You deserve to be loved...
If only you'd realise...
Your meridian's become your solitude...
And your solitude's become your depletion...
Can you see the meridian... you cursed..?
The meridian, it birthed... The death of your emotions...
Becoming a commotion... unheard...
You deserve to be reimbursed...
For all that you lost...
Meek, knee deep in fiasco...

Keep on keeping on!

CRYBABY

Seeking a farce...
You deserve to be hugged...
You deserve...
To be loved...
We all make mistakes when it's all at stake...
You only played a part that was meant to be played...
Serving a fate that was meant to be served...
You never deserved all the blame...
You deserved to heard...
You don't deserve the hate...
You deserve... To be loved...
You can't hate yourself happy...
You can't shame yourself worthy...
You chant blame of which you're unworthy...
Glistening, with the tears that you impearled...
I hope you can see...
The meridian... You cursed...

One More Smile...

You didn't listen...
I called for your name when you left...
Leaving all behind for a place in the clouds of glory, sitting besides the messiah of vain...
Leaving me in the rain... With only the longing to tail...
This breadcrumb trail of the many promises unkept...
Swept up by the whispers of the promises so noxious...
Those promises were lies...
They lie heavily upon my conscience...
Is this what it means to be conscious..?
To question the words of the dead...
No matter how absurd...
No matter how heavy they tread..?
Yet...
It's hard not to hurt over what you once said...
That, you'll be my shield...
That, I'd always be seeing...
Your smile, guaranteeing...
The safety ahead, whilst you lead...
If only life was a thing that we could all have...
And could keep...
If only my sky didn't become so dim...
When the brightest light that it had in you...
Had to leave...
I didn't listen...
You told me to be happy...
But, every corner I now turn seems to be covered in the mist and...
The reminders that you're gone catch my attention, for they seemingly glisten...
Wanting their presence known...
Wanting me reminiscing...

Keep on keeping on!

Every corner of this home...
Every corner that you once breathed in...
It seeps in...
The fear, the anger, the repent...
It all creeps in...
It's not fair...
The fact, that you had to be the one leaving...
It's the pain...
Just because I don't see it...
Doesn't mean it's not there...
It's the tears...
It resides in... Reciting my grieving...
I didn't listen...
I know you once told me to turn my imagination into a safe haven...
But the reality that now beholds me...
Is being forever lost in rumination...
A frivolous introspection...
One, devoid of all meaning...
I breathe in...
The air of despondency, ribboning my breathing...
Believing...
The despondency, guising as my sanctuary...
Has long had me imprisoned...
That, my sanctuary has now become my prison...
If optimism was an unreachable ceiling...
Then the muddy ground, I'm stuck in...
Is pessimism...
Did anyone listen..?
When my heart I cried out...
What once seemed so bright was now shrouded in clouds...
There was fear in my eyes...

Knowing your smile wouldn't last...
For your time, it ran out...
As the blur in my sight...
Gave birth to the cursed clarity...
Of the wretched reality I was endowed...
If a moment is all we are...
Then the time, it just lies...
For, this moment won't pass...
The moment I realise...
The final moment of yours...
You used your lively smile...
To rid me of aghast...
The moment I realise...
This smile will be your last...

Glass thoughts...

It's such a perfect day to watch overstay...
As it sits on the shore...
Watching me wash away...
Unable to see past the cracks...
I count all the reasons I've had...
The reasons allowing me an escape...
Cursed by the thoughts that just won't collapse...
Clad in an armour of glass...
Clad in an armour... that's vain...
Entrapped by the armour...
That's my brain...
I'm removed...
From the present...
When it's the past that has me...
When what's pre-determined, starts making me move...
Stealing the sparks, filling my room...
Stealing the warmth fuelling my heart...
Only to end up filling it with the colour of calamity...
When it's the colour of calamity that's so fucking dark..!
"My ashen heart still burns...
But, I'm breathing it's fumes..."
Stealing the destiny off of my lungs...
I've become the entity...
My entity consumes...
When the path laden with shards...
Ends up less sharper...
Than the thoughts made of glass...
When the thoughts crack and shatter...
Uttering the shards of my past...
Alas, it lasts...

Keep on keeping on!

CRYBABY

The time, it never passes...
It laughs...
Whilst, prisoning my mind eternally, passing so slow...
As it's beating even slower in my chest..!
But, I digress...
I try isolating myself from my thoughts...
Only to find myself feeling alone...
Finding that all along, it was the thoughts, isolating myself...
A transparent conundrum inside of my head...
Made apparent, when the dumb, numb thoughts made up of glass...
Became a parent that birthed, a new kind of hell...
Where the slow time, becomes slower...
Where, I forever chase the phantom...
Of loose ends...
Where the glass thoughts never shatter...
And the time, it pretends...
"BADE TUM CHALO"

I can always start tomorrow...

"I can always start tomorrow..."
I tell myself that, when it's for myself that I feel sorrow...
When It's the horror I swallow...
Alongside the pills that contain...
A partial suppression to all that follows my brain...
A prisonless cell holding all of my stress...
A prisonless cell...
That has me enchained...
"When in disguise of those pills, I suck up my pain..."
When my eyes become tainted...
And my cries become faint with...
The time that I borrowed...
When I wallow in rain and...
I'm screaming god's name, again and again...
Awaiting an answer from "him"...
As I'm waiting for an answer...
That's hollow...
As I learn, it was never an "answer"...
To hallow...
"That it'll all be okay, come tomorrow..."
"That my pain will just leave me, come tomorrow..."
That I've to pretend to be happy...
Even when it's the sadness that has me...
For it'll all be gone, come tomorrow..!
That...
"I can always start tomorrow..."
That I can always climb up from below...
That that day that's to come...
With the brightness, it'll burn...
Unlike "today", it won't numb...
Unlike "today", it won't make me fall low...

Keep on keeping on!

CRYBABY

Can I really end all of my quarrels?!
When I'm breathing "today", trying to live under the name...
Of a day that still has yet to follow..!
I can't live everyday, governed by a "tomorrow" that has my "today"...
Covered in darkness, living under its shadow..!
I'm fed up...
Being fed this advice, under the gallows..! Being told to smile, when I'm so harrowed..!
Being told such lies, whilst left breathless to writhe...
For the breath, I won't find...
Even when the breadth of the line...
Separating my "Today" from "Tomorrow"...
Becomes more and more narrow..!
I can't start over tomorrow...
It holds the unknown...
There's promises, unshown...
I can't always rely on what's shallow..!
I've still moments to spend...
I've still some time left...
To make my amends...
Mending the "today", I'd dismissed for an echo..!
I've still left a whole day to defend...
Before I wait for a "tomorrow", that's slowly caving in...
Impending, to know...
That no longer, would i be chasing it...
The "tomorrow", it knows...
That I'm the only one, on whom it could depend...
That...
No longer, would I be living a farce...
For, there's still "today" to be living in...
That...
I'll turn "today" into a garden where I could feel the wind...
Where the only sin that's ever pardoned is freely breathing in...

Messiah of porcelain...

The messiahs of clay...
They became the meaning to your short existence...
From your existential thoughts, to the clarity in your conscience...
They became all of your faith...
They became all of your resistance...
They became all of the hate...
They became the division you spread in their name and...
They became the distance...
The distance between two people...
It's this instance...
They become all that stands against their whole existence...
It's the instance, you'd forgotten...
"That your messiah was never made of porcelain..."
It all started when gods were replaced by "prophets"...
When their own beliefs became the god's...
When your faith started becoming paper thin...
When your faith started being used for profit...
When the thinnest thread of amity became the biggest luxury you could wear...
When you heard your fleeting sanity tremble in fear...
When you swore your own vanity, no memories of impair...
When you lost that precious part of thee...
You'd hold onto so dear...
When you forgot, your god was never porcelain...
When you forgot...
That your problems were never the god's to hear...
When you forgot...
That your burdens were never the god's to bear...
You're the heir...
The heir, to the gods... you created...
Their ideals, their thoughts...

Keep on keeping on!

CRYBABY

They're yours... To be tainted...
The words of the sacred...
Never came from the "sacred"...
The love and the greatness...
Was never native to the "greatest"...
Yet, it doesn't mean the hatred...
Was ever there to begin with...
You pray with all your heart...
You believe in a god of clay and...
You fight for what you believe in...
You fight for what you "think" the truth's in...
You fight for what you "believe" is true...
But, have you ever entertained the thought that...
Maybe, God does not believe in "you"..?
Maybe, the Messiah of porcelain...
Isn't the one you should pursue...
Maybe God won't give you love just because you want him to...
Maybe, if it's the love you want...
The love's got to come from you...
"BADE TUM CHALO"

Meaning...

Remember...
To be aware of your potential, is to open your eyes...
To remember a smile, working against the ticking time...
To speak your own mind, with all of it's hidden insight...
To try and not search for what's hidden...
In sight...
For what's hidden in sight... Is the site of all spite... It's...
"Meaning"...
It's the Messiah you look for...
With a smile you latch onto its feet...
Letting it drag you further and further...
It's when your future, once filled with "wonder"...
Falls, crumbling under... The confines of blunder...
Yet, you smile... As you continue to suffer...
While inside of your heart, you're stuck screaming bloody murder...
You hide from the love... Deeming it a bane to your "peace"...
When it's still unheard of...
You hedge your bloody bets...
Pledging an audience with your regrets...
You search through all your words...
For all the "meaning"... They never held...
It's inside of your head...
Where you try and frame your own self...
Framing your own self...
For all the damage you never dealt..!
Yet, you knelt..!
You knelt to the voice, promising clarity to the doubts that you still harbour...
"Every moment's and opportunity in disguise..."
Yet, you let the "meaning" behind those words dampen all your ardour...

Keep on keeping on!

CRYBABY

You seek an escape from your past... Knowing well, that the cause of freedom may cost you to become a martyr...

Yet, you barter..?!

You barter with life for all the "meaning" it hides...

Knowing in spite, that there's no "truth" that's inside...

Knowing all well, that the meaning...

It lies...

You know it all well...

Yet, you chase it...

For respite..!

Remember...

To be aware of your potential, is to close your own eyes...

To remember a smile, that ages well with time...

To not waste your own life on the meaningless lies...

To live in the truth...

And not be meaningless inside...

Whilst, the only meaning you find...

Becomes the meaning behind...

The smile...

That you hide...

Suicidal angel...

I did it to myself...
I knew, that it'd be painful...
I fight my mental health...
With the demons, that I fabled...
I threw my wings in hell...
I fell...
A suicidal angel...
I carve onto my skin, the number of days...
That never pardoned me...
I sing with my knife, the lullaby of my woes...
As it's the song that it sings, during its sharpening...
I find my peace, hidden in the shadows...
As the room, I'm locked in...
Starts breathing...
I ruminate in my mind...
Finding meaning in all that's hollow...
Only to find myself hanging...
From this dark ceiling...
"I've seen enough to be blind eyed"...
As the soulless room, it mocks me...
Animating itself with the echoes...
Of my cries, deemed disheartening...
I fall free, from my feelings...
For, I feel the room... moving...
Moving more than I...
"When, the only corner that's ever answered to me... Starts darkening..."
I reckon myself, battle hardened...
But, the battles... They weren't so hard on me...
These shackles, they scar... For, I'm living a farce...
And if it's all just a farce, then why do these scars...

"Really" burden me..?
I'm drowning in the well...
Of my tears... They're so shameful...
I find it hard to tell...
If towards me, they're faithful...
There's no one else to blame...
But, me...
A suicidal angel...
I did it to myself...
I fell...
A suicidal angel...
Banished into hell...
I dwell...
A suicidal angel...

ME...

I don't feel safe... In my head...
I see the faces... of the dead...
They wish, it was me... In their stead...
I let the guilt... Chastise me...
My vision's... lost my trust...
It blinded me... it gave me rust...
Were my decisions always so rushed..?
Or did I let the hindsight... Blind me..?
Over and over, I go...
Over the thoughts that make "myself" erode...
Revising horror, these visions follow me home...
I wonder why they despise me..?
Oh, I can't see..!
I say...
Oh..!
I can't see..!
All I know...
Is, I can breathe...
Once, the guilt... No longer defines me...
Once, I let myself find "me"...
I can't breathe... in this pain...
I hear the voices say my name...
They whisper... all of their hate...
Into my ears... They surround me..!
I wish... I could prove...
To myself... that maybe, I'm the one, construed...
In a light, wronged by abuse...
With the sight... That has confined me...
Oh, I can't see..!
I say...

Oh..!
I can't see..!
All I know...
Is, I can breathe...
Once, the guilt... No longer defines me...
Once, I let myself find "me"...
I'm stuck battling my attrition...
In this battle of attrition...
"I can't take anymore of the fact that I still can take a lot more..."
Reckon, I've to set "me" free...
If I wish to be home...
Reckon, I've to tell myself that over and over... in a low roar...
Reckon, I've to learn to be "me"...
Reckon, I've a soul to restore...
I might just be able to see...
For, I've still a soul... To restore...

Keep on keeping on!

Home...

Somebody call my home...
The one, I lost in obsession...
Somebody call my home...
The one, borne of fiction...
I'll chase it till I'm gone...
I've no will to question...
I'll break through, on my own...
I'll find my true reason...
Somebody call my home...
I've lost all my passion...
Nobody called me home...
Reckon, I've to make a confession...
The "home" that I adored...
It never existed, even in imagination...
I worshipped the unknown...
I worshipped my own... slow recession...
I worshipped mystique...
I worshipped, alone...
I worshipped a home, never shown...
I worshipped the bleak...
I worshipped the worship I'd feed...
To the sins I'd repeat, ever since my pursuit of the "meek"...
I see...
What I sought wasn't a "home", but belief...
What I sought was a mere peek at relief...
What I sought through the words that I'd speak...
To the beats of the heart that I steeled...
Was a world where the "world" let's me breathe...
"A world, where the home calls for me"...

Keep on keeping on!

CRYBABY

Somebody call my home...
I've lost all my obsession...
Somebody call me home...
The home doesn't have to be "heaven"...
Somebody call me home...
My life...
It hasn't been a journey...
But, a confession...

Keep on keeping on!

Mirror

The rain, in my skies just won't end...
The words, that I scar myself with, are always ripe for ensnare...
Alone, I try seeking the end...
I'm home, when I'm the only one to blame, when I'm in pain...
So, I wake myself up...
As the one in the mirror, checks his own pulse...
With The blood in my eyes...
With the sweat in my clothes...
I see the one, who's red eyed...
I see the one, so far... Yet close...
"I'm the only one stressed..."
"I'm the only one tired of feeling so strained..."
I tell myself that...
But, the one in the mirror suggests, it isn't that strange...
He says, he lives in my brain...
That, we bare a name... The same...
He says, I'm not, "one in a million"...
But, I'm the only "me" in billions...
That I'm him...
He tries sharing my pain...
He tries seeming, the same... He's here...
If there's a noose on my neck...
He'd too, be waiting the end... With me...
With a hole in my chest...
But, a smile on my face... I see...
There's someone in the mirror...
There's someone, that cares...
There's someone, who isn't... Yet free...
There's someone in the mirror...
Someone trapped in the snares...
There's someone, who's no-one... But me...

CRYBABY

Mirror

"There's someone...
Who's no-one, but me..."
Im relieved...
knowing the fact that it's in the mirror, I see my past retract...
That it's in the mirror, I still see a self, intact...
That it's in the mirror, I see a little clearer, Through all that's brittle, abused, yet abstract..!
That, inside the mirror...
Resides a self that mirrors, the self I haven't yet entrapped...
Inside the mirror, resides a self with errors, I'd love to fucking adapt...
I breathe in...
I rest my soul...
I'm worth it...
"I can be loved..."
It's breaking...
From the cracks, long formed...
The mirror's breaking...
Guess, it can't keep love...

Keep on keeping on!

Snowflake

One more night alone....
Deafened, I'll be coming home...
One more night, on my own...
This traffic greets me when I'm all alone...
One more night to own...
Before I realise, she's long gone...
One more night corrodes...
I know the snowflake loved it when I'd come back home...
Listen close...
Is it hope..?
Beating, without rest...
Though the heart, with its sharp teeth in my chest...
Or the heartbeat, in the breast...
Of the broken and bruised...
The one, feeling beaten and used...
Kneeling as a pawn, to the face of the evil...
One masked up, longing to consume...
That fake fuck that's followed us all the way from the womb..!
I apologise...
Because I couldn't see the pain in your damn eyes...
Because I couldn't tell, beneath the smiles were your damned cries...
Because I let you leave...
Couldn't see you fleeing with all the pain hiding underneath your face, in plain sight..!
All that anguish...
Filled her life in between the phases, her mind slept...
Lost in conquest...
Tried finding peace, a life serene, in the ocean, her eyes wept...
Listen close...
It isn't hope...

CRYBABY

It's the heartbreak... it's the stress...
Over a heartbeat, in rest...
Earthed, yet beating in the mist...
While, my heart's still bleeding reminisce, I'm a mess..!
I'm amiss..!
It's the cries of the dead and the vanquished..!
For, the love in her heart was the answer...
And I'd drop it on the world, as an anchor...
Giving hope to the damned and the depressed, I'll...
Try and preserve her idea of peace and an ideal world...
Never lonely when you're flowing through my mind, girl...
I apologise...
Because I couldn't see the rain in your damned skies..!
Because I couldn't see...
What you sought was an escape from your heart in between the constraints, straining your mind with your faint cries..!
I... Can only apologise...
Soon I'd realise...
Realise, that it was never hope...
But, the sound of a night... Alone...
Realise, that it was never hope...
That, I used to calm my entire hell with...
A flake of snow...

Half asleep...

I broke...
Through my sleep...
I woke...
Half asleep...
It's pitch dark...
Living under these sheets...
It's pitch dark...
Living a life, one so meek...
Rise up...
And stay there a while...
Times' flying...
Contemplate on your life...
"The day's dying..."
"Get up and just try..."
"I'm trying..."
"I know how much I've tried..."
It's the morning's fault...
It hates my will to live...
The more we talk...
The more I will, it's leave...
The more we talk...
The less I will, It here...
I broke...
Through my sleep...
I woke...
Half asleep...
Realising it isn't the slumber I need...

Keep on keeping on!

CRYBABY

I wonder why is it the slumber, I heed...
Torn asunder, my soul... spells out the blunder, I read...
I number my days, the more encumbered I feel...
The colder I get, the more sombre I bleed...
Under the shower's when I honour my tears...
Under the shower spawns the cowardice, borne of my fears...
It's under the shower, I converse with the unclear...
It's under the shower, I try closing my ears...
Closing my ears, to all these fucking voices I hear..!
I broke...
Through my sleep...
I woke...
Half asleep...
I rose...
Procrastinated a while...
I rose...
Anew, and I tried...
It's pitch dark...
For another day has now died...
It's pitch dark...
Another day has now died...

Clarity...

"So if I escape...
Will my pain go away..?"
They ask themselves the questions needless to say...
A walk in their minds makes them wonder...
Never realising it was their minds that they plundered...
They do have a home, but there's nobody there...
Left with nothing, but only a life to be spared...
they stay in this "room", where they come to realise...
That leaving this place, won't make them "alive"...
That everything ever, has just been a big fucking lie..!
That, they're now rendered...
With not a choice...
But to die...
So...
They sever their bonds...
Taking the wheel...
Of the long lost control...
They do it all for the clarification that they've never known...
Giving themselves the rest...
They reckon their goal...
The feelings Oppressed, pressed, stressed...
Burst out their chests, along with their blissless breaths, never blessed..!
So, they pay for their ambitions with repent!?
Fleeing their lives with doubts still in their heads!?
This' how their stories come to an end!?
Starting with dull blades on their wrists..?
Ending with a look at the rope...
Then a jump... Forever lost in the mist..?
While we play pretend, picking these fucking daffodils... That's the gist!?
Their bodies were starved...

CRYBABY

To keep their feet in the air...
All they needed was a slip...
Their stories stopped with their hearts...
To keep their feet in the air...
All they needed was the rope's tight grip...
I tried holding their ghosts...
They slipped right through my fingertips...
I tried holding their ghosts
They slipped right through my fingertips...
They did it all for some clarity...
I hope, they got what they were looking for...
When alone...
"It" was their god...
With them being the devil, resenting all...
They did it all for some clarity...
I hope, they got what they were looking for...
When alone...
"It" was their god...
With them being the devil, resenting all...
They did it all for some clarity...
I hope, they got what they were looking for...
When alone...
"It" was their god...
With them being the devil, resenting all...
With them being the fallen, resenting all...

I see the sunset...

I see the sunset...
I feel the warmth, end...
There's no more to pretend...
For I've witnessed the horizons bend...
I didn't wake up early...
I just never slept...
The sun, it never left me...
But, kept chasing behind my head...
I won't wake, before I'm left alone...
By this pretentious warmth, I'm never shown...
I see the sunset...
I feel the warmth end...
I heal from all, the day dealt...
As I watch the cold settle in...
I part my ways with the crooked reality...
Only to find myself stranded on the horizonless beach...
In my dream, where there's no clarity...
forever unnoticed... Forever unseen...
I lie there, lifeless...
With life being what I beseech...
Yet, feeling alive without life...
I wonder what "life" truly means..?
The sand here harms me with it's warmth...
The trees here warn me with their mourns...
Of all that's swarming towards these shores...
It's the rays that scorn me, never leaving me alone...
I see the sunset...
I feel the warmth, end...
I'd let my yawn out...
As long as there's no more to pretend...
I see the sunset...
I see my day end...

Envy

Owing debt to despair, I feel so deprived...
I envy the light on those, I despise...
I envy the fears clouding their minds...
I envy the fact it makes them alive...
I envy the breaths they breathe...
I envy the fact they sleep...
I envy the fact they feel..!
I envy them, so to speak...
I reside in a soulless pit...
I drift aside, without a grip...
I slip, falling to where the devil lives...
The only rise, my soul finds...
Is an escape to a sky made of abyss...
An escape from which I can't run away...
I try my best to erase...
This numbness, made of memories unmade...
This numbness, making my memories fade...
I see, black skies...
Clouded with white lies...
I'd rather be...
Befriending the enemies, I envy...
Than pretending to play pretend with my insecurities...
I won't allow myself the happiness that, I've spied for all eternity...
As the ground under me, crumbling...
Further crumbles me...
I see, a black demise...
Shrouded with white smiles...
I'd rather sleep...
Attending to the sombre dark, for all eternity...
Than spending my days, being a witness to all my atrocities...

CRYBABY

I won't denounce the weariness, my shoulders are too numb to feel...
As the sounds that circle me, start mumbling...
All, that burdens me...
I see, black skies...
Clouded with white lies...
I'd rather be...
Dead, than haunted by the fewer few...
I envy...

Keep on keeping on!

Orphan

Asylums for my breathing...
Hold the misfortunes, I'm concealing...
I sigh my hums in kneeling...
I'm Orphaned by my feelings...
I orphan all that heals me...
I often find me peeling...
My poisoned skin, revealing...
The exertion I've been bleeding...
My importance is receding... Believe me...
Orphaned by all meaning... I'm fleeting...
I cry and run to the pleading...
Please, free me...
From these asylums that've prisoned my breathing...
I find silence, in my screaming...
There's solace, in the lost meaning...
These sirens, they've been scheming...
My horizons, they're deceiving...
I lighten my heart's beating...
When I find my light to be leaving...
"There's might in all this, nothing"...
A lie, I find being pleasing...
My sight has just been screening...
The cries, i once believed in...
My eyes, they've been weakened...
By the silent faults, they're heeding...
Time flies, it's truly unhealing...
Under the asylums for my breathing...
I author myself dreaming, the unseen...
It's rather demeaning...

Keep on keeping on!

CRYBABY

I harbour my self-esteem, gleaming...
I glamour my misdealings....

I digress from what's seemingly redeeming...
I'm hammered by my own hearing....
I've orphaned all I've been fearing...
In this asylum, for my feelings...
Asylums for my breathing...
Hold the misfortunes, I'm concealing...
I sigh my hums in kneeling...
I'm Orphaned by my feelings...
I orphan all that heals me...
I orphan all that hears me...
I find myself, grieving...
In these asylums for my breathing...

Keep on keeping on!

Anxiety

It was a bright white night, serving me with eerie...
On a plate, cold with an epiphany...
When the walls around me, started caving in...
Oh, I breathed in...
I breathed in...
I breathed in...
The night's sly shine... It creeped and crawled under my skin...
Sinking it's pasty bright teeth in my flesh...
I'm fetched, by the rusty hooks it used to reel me in...
Becoming my messiah, a sovereign of my dreams...
A king to my desires, akin to my lost esteem...
It was then...
When my dreams started controlling my everything...
It was then...
When I questioned, being born a child to my destiny...
"I just needed time..."
"I just needed love..."
I tell myself, as I continue to fall...
"Aren't I still alive..?"
"Isn't this all, just a bluff..?"
I slap myself anew, to wake up...
"So, did I win..?"
"Is it gone, my blame..?"
I ask myself, while I'm still caving in...
"Guess, such is life..."
"Guess, such is fate..."
Oppressed and hurt...
I feel the hate...
But, wait...
Can you blame..?

Keep on keeping on!

CRYBABY

Anxiety

It was a bright white night, serving me with eerie...
On a plate, cold with an epiphany...
When the walls around me, started caving in...
Oh, I breathed in...
I breathed in...
I breathed in...
I look into the abyss...
It looks back at me...
I guess, the both of us think, "Life's fucking funny"
As the pulse in my neck...
Begins diminishing...
With a smirk...
I breathe in...
I breathe in...

Keep on keeping on!

Insomnia

I'm taking my demons out for a ride, I promise it won't take long...

Sleep's such a silly disguise that I'd hide under... Leaving behind, all that is wrong...

I know, my time and my space is melting, it's all blurry... But, I'll get on...

It's getting hard to tell day from a day...

Wide awake, I want help... To move on...

An Abel, rather capable, of being cabled to reality, stuck as a mere mislabel to his own Bible's fables... Labelled stable, on paper... tapered his irritable lids to his forehead in horrid with the stapler he borrowed from the hatred he swallowed in his despaired sorrow...

I'd like to author my concreted state into running water...

But my troubles always seem to double as I fumble and tumble under the dark circling my eyes, coupled with grumble...

I crumble, as the gazes I face, rebuttal in rumble.

I'm humbled, as soon as I stumble off the bubble, I once cuddled the thoughts left supple in the cold in...

I'm folding, wondering why my insomnia couldn't have been more subtle...

Left unshut for days, my dried eyes, wide awake, in a daze... Dream of shit that's irrelevant... I lose my being's relevance as my fears seemingly appear benevolent...

I keep thinking... I keep thinking... I keep thinking of...

Everything...

Everything that's a phantom...

Everything that's fucking nothing...

Is this my true element..?

An insomniac state, eloquent in elegant malevolence...

A celibate of sleep, desolate as a pessimistic celebrant of his own negligence, under peace's defecit, roaming as a revenant, sheltered

CRYBABY

under his unending thought's venemous vehemont resident...

My eyes are bleeding as I keep counting the sheep that bleat in a bleak weep heeding to the deeds reaped by the heart, beating a beaten plea, reeking of a sleepless soul's complete and utter defeat... I'm depleted...

I can't fucking sleep...

I can't fucking sleep...

I'm taking my demons out for a ride, I promise it won't take long...

Sleep's such a silly disguise that I'd hide under... Leaving behind, all that is wrong...

I know, my time and my space is melting, it's all blurry... But, I'll get on...

It's getting hard to tell day from a day...

Wide awake, I want help... To move on...

Lost Guardian

Broken...
I'm bleeding out through my heart and my eyes...
Hoping...
You'd forgive me, not being able to hold back my cries...
Woken...
In hopes that I could see you alive...
Stolen...
I've lost the only friend holding my life...
Never knew how much you meant to me...
Till I couldn't sleep without you in my dreams...
Life's not the same without you at my side...
Promise, I would wipe my tears and follow behind...
Promise, to fight my fears and to make the time...
So, please come back and take me to the light...
Please... Come back and take me to the light...
Never knew how much you meant to me...
Till I couldn't sleep without you in my dreams...
I can't tell the difference from being asleep and awake...
Wouldn't know if I was loosing my patience, my unconscious conscience...
Or my unfeeling faith...
Find me a new made grave...
Your death left me a dead man...
Cold, I've been up for days...
My body is numb... I can't feel the pain
Missing the warmth, I can't escape the rain...
Never knew how much you meant to me...
Till I couldn't sleep without you in my dreams...
I'm lost without your love...
Come, burn away my flaws...

Keep on keeping on!

CRYBABY

I didn't just lose a guardian...
I lost a part of my soul...
Another lonely day...
Blemishing, while I reminisce the memories that you have left...
Would rather die insane...
Than people telling me that my life is graced...
Find me a new made grave...
Your death left me a dead man...
Cold, I've been up for days...
My body is numb... I can't feel the pain
Missing the warmth, I can't escape the rain...
I'm lost without your love...
Wouldn't trust my faith for even once...
You were the only one...
That'd burn away my flaws...
My head's about to burst...
Without your warm hand above..
My heart's bleeding out...
In a corner at my home...
Why did you leave me alone..?
Was it something, I did wrong..?
I didn't just lose a guardian...
I lost a part of my soul...
I feel so fucking lost...
Where have you gone..?
I'm so fucking lost...
Where have you gone..?

Keep on keeping on!

When The Moonlight Tunrned Scarlet ...

Under the oak tree...
When the moonlight turned scarlet...
This despair brimmed cesspit...
Appeared to be less of a harlot...
Plundered my soul clean...
Till the borrowed bright, once dullish...
Through my crimsoned eyes, was leered, to be a bit more worth it...
Adhered to it's lust, of wanting itself sculpted...
By the gaze, bathed in saffron...
Of the man that gored his hermit...
It was under the oak tree...
When my sight yearned a bright red...
It was under the oak tree...
When the moonlight turned scarlet...
The cron, crowned with blood...
Remained unbroken, but concussed...
Had a stream of red, voyage...
Down his brows, up from his head...
The torn hound, recovered...
From the derange he'd motioned into a rush...
Past the gleam, bred of carnage...
Frowned a growl, birthed from this, now "blissed" hell...
Maybe, he was wasting time..?
Hazy, was his state of mind...
He'd been a little crazy, lately... Yet he managed staying alive...
Dazy, he dared a dive inside his head...
Found himself, with knuckles dusted in blood... Hanging by a thread...
Yet, everything seemed to be worth it..?
Perhaps, all for the moonlight that he'd sculpted...
Under the oak tree...

Keep on keeping on!

CRYBABY

When the moonlight turned scarlet...
This despair brimmed cesspit...
Appeared to be less of a harlot...
Blundered, even a sold dream...
Till the sorrowed plight, once rubbish...
Though my sin fed eyes... was seared...
Into a sculpt, more charlotte...

Crybaby

Once, drowned a crybaby...
In a gutter of her own tears...
A flood bounced awry in daisy...
Tinked the fluster hummed past her ears...
The fronts, frowned upon the hazy...
Binned the flutter of her mourned cheers...
The cunts roundabout a bailey...
Sling a raze, wretchedly uttered in their brone leers...
Passive obsession...
With the blade in her hands...
Defensive offender...
Killed the hate to make amends...
Rancid possession...
Of a peer in resent...
Flaccid recession...
Of a fate in descent...
Offensive defence...
Fancied self-violence...
Drew on her wrists, so her heartbeat would go silent...
She played the victim, and he played the saint...
Rue risen mist, drove her to reap a Cain in relent...
She craved the ritz, and he caved to the bane...
Don't you fucking dare...
Let him catch her in pain...
Alone, drops a mucky tear...
Longing to hatch a scarlet rain...
The scars on her body...
Couldn't just be kissed away...
The lark, borne of shoddy...
Couldn't just be dissed ablaze...

Keep on keeping on!

CRYBABY

Offensive defence...
Fancied self-violence...
Drew on her wrists, so her heartbeat would go silent...
She played the victim, and he played the saint...
Once, drowned a crybaby...
In a flood filled with disdain...

A Valentine Blur

I sold my soul for plastic...
I scold my ghoul, the Baptist...
I rolled my dule mule's liver for breakfast...
Foretold my blight, a tragedy rather drastic...
Fill my eyes with a grimed spur...
Till the day I die, a valentine blur...
I hold my role, a loft for all that's hectic...
Before, befalls thy vore, a croft for all that's wilted...
Kill the rye quip, one that survived the dull...
Live with my cries until, the shun has materialized with rud...
Trim my life's hilt, donned with a rhymed slur...
Till the day I die, a valentine blur...
The grin I unsheathed, rendered me, a wolf in fever...
The blood rinsed on my teeth, gushed from the much tender meat, of a Rudolph wrung in shivers...
The clot, pissed in a flurry, rushed from the once fendered kidneys, of the now, foul sunk Oliver...
The red, curried in hurry, flushed from the runt's slandered beliefs, spread and bowed, before the stout lunk's quiver...
What I yearned wasn't as much...
Even so, what I earned wasn't enough...
Now, destined to die a valentine blur...
I wait, for what's to end it all...
The plastic lies, I traded my life for...

BLESSING

Noose Like Necklace

I hung my angel with a necklace...
A noose jewelled around its neck... The mule mused, denounced in debt...
A poor fool's background in wreck... as a cruel wolf, resound in wretch...
I hung my angel with a necklace...
What the fuck do you really know about me?
Say, will you ask my ever-changing perspective..?
Break, the sill casketing this deranging heretic...
Will you ask, those poor curb-stomped cunts, with mugs fashioned in saffron..?
Or will it be those moonshine eyes, he once rationed..?
Until you task the crow's crumbled and wronged lunts, rick runts'll come crashing in arson...
A sour quill's fit reshows his vanaheim lies, the ones rumped in fashion...
Don't hate it when you hear my name...
A Crone satiated, when I feared the tame...
I hung my angel with a necklace...
I sunk the dangers, frilled with the reckless...
The next time you go down on lady fate's clit, detest the taste of my dick...
Berate that crest of a prick...
Serrate the rest of his sly ritz...
Lest wanting to witness his gaze menace laced...
Don't hate it when you hear my name...
Even though I hung my angel with a necklace...

Keep on keeping on!